DRONES

DRONES

MARTIN J. DOUGHERTY

SCHOLASTIC INC.

This edition published by Scholastic Inc., 557 Broadway, New York, NY 10012 by arrangement with Amber Books Ltd.

SCHOLASTIC and associated logos are trademarks of Scholastic Inc.

Distributed by Scholastic Canada Ltd., Markham, Ontario
Scholastic New Zealand Ltd., Greenmount, Auckland

10 9 8 7 6 5 4 3 2 1   14 15 16 17

ISBN 978-0-545-66476-9

Editorial and design by
Amber Books Ltd
74–77 White Lion Street
London N1 9PF
United Kingdom
www.amberbooks.co.uk

Project Editor: Sarah Uttridge
Design: Zoë Mellors
Picture Research: Terry Forshaw

Printed in Shenzhen, China by Hung Hing Offset

First printing, August 2014

CONTENTS

INTRODUCTION

There are some places where people can't go, or where it's far too dangerous. Modern technology gives us the ability to see, work, and fight in these places without placing people in danger by using "drones"—remotely operated vehicles.

There are many kinds of drones. Some fly in the air and others operate in water. Most are designed for a specific task, but some can carry out a wide range of jobs. What they all have in common is that they allow an operator to carry out complex tasks at a distance, without moving from his or her console.

Military drones are mostly used to gather information and sometimes to attack targets with missiles. They can often sneak into areas that are heavily defended, using advanced stealth technology (making them invisible to radar) or just by being really small. Civilian drones are also often used to gather information, usually by using cameras to send images back to base. They can be used for everything from making maps to finding out how fast a forest fire is spreading. Some specialist drones can carry out scientific experiments high in the air or deep underwater.

In the Danger Zone

Drones can be sent into places where it would simply be too dangerous for humans to go. The RQ-4 Global Hawk is illustrated opposite—this drone is used for surveillance and supports military missions worldwide.

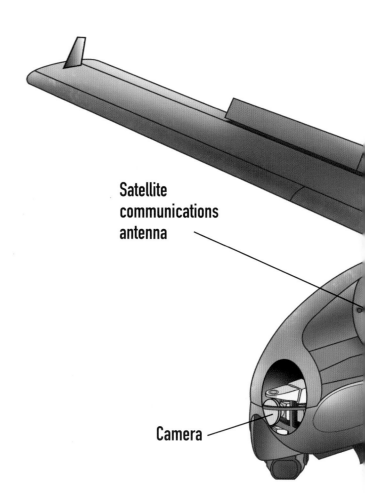

Satellite communications antenna

Camera

RQ-4 Global Hawk

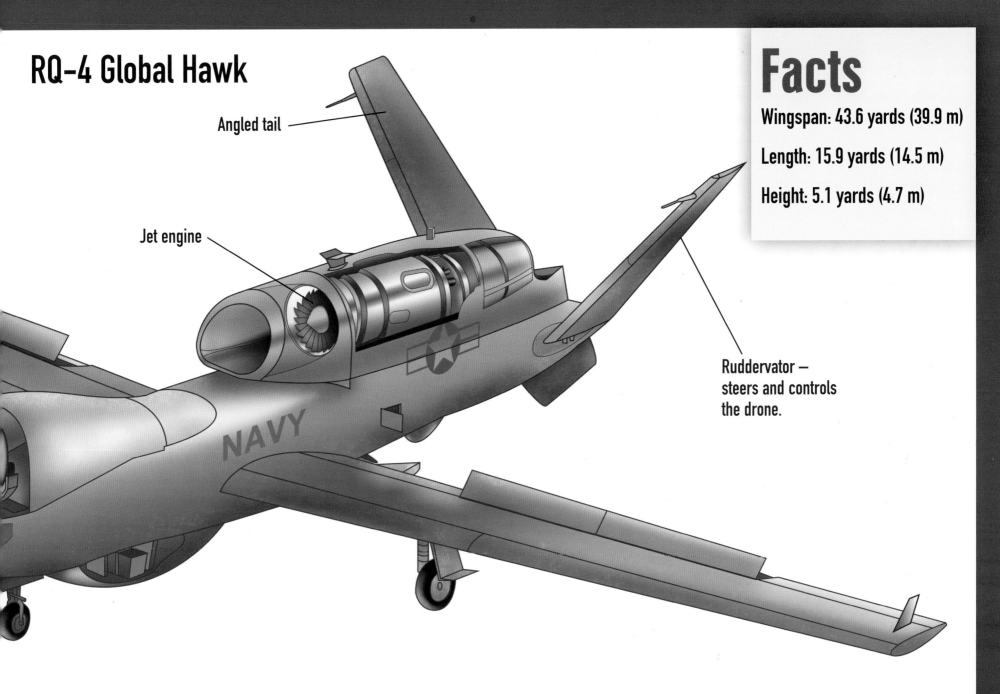

Angled tail

Jet engine

Facts

Wingspan: 43.6 yards (39.9 m)

Length: 15.9 yards (14.5 m)

Height: 5.1 yards (4.7 m)

Ruddervator — steers and controls the drone.

NAVY

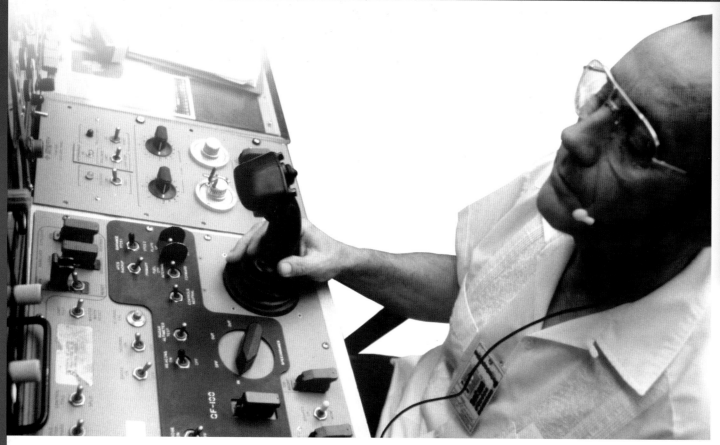

Facts

Drone operators go to war sitting down in a comfortable chair with plenty of coffee handy, but theirs is a very difficult job all the same.

Drone Operators

Drones are designed to be operated from a distance. In some cases, that distance is quite short, but it is possible to control a drone flying over Afghanistan or Iraq from the United States. You need some very good communications equipment to do that.

Many drones are operated using a joystick and pedals, much like an aircraft. The operator cannot feel what the drone is doing, which makes the job tricky.

Some drones are operated by a two-person team, with one of the crew controlling cameras and other instruments while the pilot concentrates on putting the drone where it needs to be. It is important that they are highly trained and have the right natural skills.

Drone operators spend a lot of time looking at featureless expanses of desert or other very boring scenes, yet must be instantly alert to spot a hidden enemy vehicle or unit, or to respond to a sudden threat. Where the drone is operating in a war zone, they may have to witness highly unpleasant scenes that most people never see.

Did You Know?

Flying a drone is not like playing a game. It is tiring to have to concentrate closely all the time, and a single mistake can cost lives.

A good team can get the best out of their drone, helping to find the enemy and, in some cases, attacking them.

MQ-1 PREDATOR

The Predator is one of the most famous military drones. It has a strange-looking downward-pointing tail and is driven by a propeller at the rear. When it was developed in the early 1990s the Predator was not armed, but today's drones can carry two Hellfire missiles. Hellfire missiles are very accurate; they are guided to the target by a laser beam.

Predator is a MALE drone (medium-altitude, long-endurance). This means it can fly fairly high and stay on station (in the target area) for a long time.

Facts

Predator drones are used by the armed forces of several countries and also by the CIA. They can carry weapons as well as surveillance cameras.

One of the challenges facing the design team was the need to create a quiet engine so that the enemy would not hear the Predator approaching. The Predator is able to sneak into places that the enemy thinks are safe and then launch a surprise attack. It can be used for close air support, firing missiles at enemy bunkers to assist US ground troops, and can hit a moving target.

The Predator has been used as the basis for other drones, some of them military and others used for many different civilian purposes.

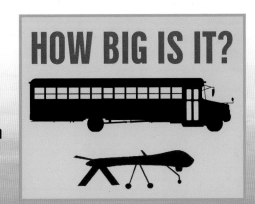

HOW BIG IS IT?

Did You Know?

The Predator can carry a smaller drone to the target area, then carry out its own mission after launching it.

MQ-9 REAPER

The Reaper was developed from the MQ-1 Predator. It looks very similar, but the tail section is different. The Reaper has two fins slanted upward and one pointing straight down. It has a vastly more powerful engine than the Predator.

Missiles

Sensor

Did You Know?

The Reaper can remain on station for three times as long as a Predator and can carry out missions over a far greater distance.

A Reaper can be operated by different teams while some of its operators rest, making very long missions possible without exhausting the original crew.

One possible future purpose for Reaper drones is to carry specialist weapons to eliminate enemy radar, guns, and missile systems to clear a path for manned aircraft.

HOW BIG IS IT?

Facts

The Reaper can carry up to 14 missiles. It has six external pylons that can carry laser-guided bombs and missiles, GPS-guided bombs, or Stinger and Sidewinder air-to-air missiles.

As well as being capable of attack missions, the Reaper is an excellent sensor platform, equipped with various cameras, thermal imaging equipment, a laser rangefinder, and radar. It is used in US Homeland Security operations, monitoring coastlines and long borders that would be difficult to patrol at ground level.

The United States and a number of allied nations have also explored the use of Reaper drones at sea, as part of anti-piracy and maritime security operations. It has also been approved for use in disaster situations, where it could search for survivors and assess damage to remote areas with its cameras and thermal imagers.

MQ-1C GRAY EAGLE

The Gray Eagle drone was also developed from the Predator. It looks more or less the same, but its wings are longer. Its electronics are better, making the Gray Eagle more likely to survive if something goes wrong with its control systems.

Gray Eagle is built as individual modules, making it easy to swap components to change missions or to replace damaged ones.

Gray Eagle was originally called Warrior, then Sky Warrior, before being given its official service name.

Facts

Gray Eagle can carry four Hellfire missiles and has hardpoints on the wings to carry a range of equipment including sensors and weapons.

U.S.ARMY
WARRIOR

AERONAUTICAL SYSTEMS

HOW BIG IS IT?

Gray Eagle's missions include strikes against enemy targets, using either Hellfire missiles or the GBU-44 Viper Strike bomb. This uses GPS guidance to glide to the target after the drone releases it, then makes its final attack assisted by laser targeting. It can even hit a moving vehicle.

As well as attacking the enemy with precision weapons, the Gray Eagle can also conduct reconnaissance (searching an area) and provides its users with a quick way to assess the damage caused by an IED (improvised explosive device) or other enemy action. The Gray Eagle drone is equipped to intercept enemy radio signals and to carry out electronic warfare missions where they interfere with enemy radio and radar by broadcasting a powerful jamming signal.

Did You Know?

The Gray Eagle drone can stay airborne for over 30 hours and can fly at altitudes of up to 9,843 yards (9,000 m).

The US Army plans to deploy 11 Gray Eagles, but some officers have said that they want drones in every army division because they are so useful.

AVENGER AND SEA AVENGER

The Avenger drone is part of the same "family" of drones as the Predator and Reaper, but uses a jet engine that makes it more than twice as fast as a Predator. It is a large and expensive drone, but very capable.

The Avenger carries its weapons in an internal bay. This helps minimize its radar signature and also improves both speed and fuel economy.

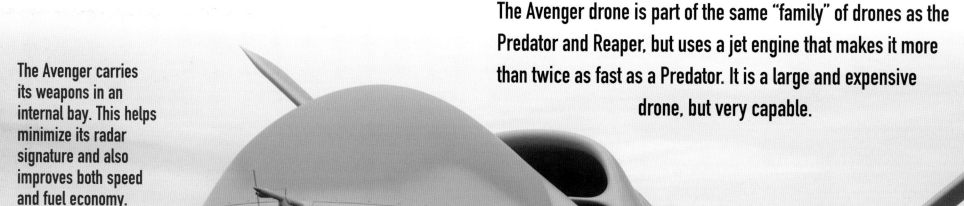

Facts

The Avenger uses an advanced stealthy design, including an S-shaped engine exhaust that helps conceal the thermal (heat) signature from its powerful jet engine.

The Avenger is a large and expensive drone, designed for speed and to move around without being detected. This enables it to operate in areas where the enemy has good air defenses. In some ways it is more like a full-sized aircraft (just without a pilot on board) than a drone. A version that can be used from aircraft carriers is also under development. This new model is known as Sea Avenger.

Avenger drones have advanced sensors and can launch Hellfire missiles and guided bombs ranging from the GBU-39 Small Diameter Bomb to large 1,984-pound (900 kg) weapons.

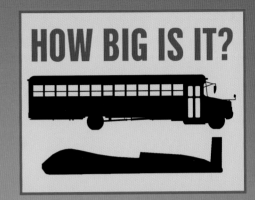

HOW BIG IS IT?

Drones like the Avenger cannot yet replace manned aircraft, but there are many people who think that one day they might.

Did You Know?

The Avenger is almost twice as fast as a Reaper drone. It can fly at heights of over 9.3 miles (15 km) and can stay airborne for 18 hours or more.

FURY 1500

Fury 1500 is a much smaller drone than the Avenger or even Predator. It is launched from a pneumatic (compressed air) launcher and does not need a runway. This makes it effective for use aboard small ships or in remote areas.

The small size and quiet engine of the drone make it unlikely that the enemy will detect it.

The Fury 1500 can be set up with payload (the load an aircraft carries) bays either above or below the main fuselage, or under the wings.

HOW BIG IS IT?

Did You Know?

The Fury 1500 is recovered using a net. This means it needs no landing facilities at all, and can be picked up on land or at sea.

Facts

Using a delta-wing configuration and a propeller at the rear, the Fury 1500 can carry three times its own empty weight.

The Fury 1500's engine generates electrical power for the drone's systems and can deliver enough to run even powerful systems such as electronic warfare jammers.

The Fury 1500 is designed for ISR (intelligence, surveillance, and reconnaissance) and EW (electronic warfare) missions. Its design allows different packages of instruments and equipment to be swapped out as needed, and the drone can carry up to three different packages at once.

Its range of 1,500 nautical miles (1,726 miles; 2,778 km) and endurance of over 15 hours allow the drone to remain on station for a long period, permitting near-constant surveillance of an area of interest with just a handful of drones. The drone has shielded electronics, which makes it hard for the enemy to jam its transmissions or interfere with its mission.

RQ-4 GLOBAL HAWK

Global Hawk was developed to fly at extremely high altitudes and undertake long missions. It is not a combat platform designed to launch missiles at the enemy, but instead undertakes long-range reconnaissance missions over land or sea.

HOW BIG IS IT?

Facts

Global Hawk can stay aloft for more than 35 hours and operates at an altitude of almost 12 miles (20 km). This is high enough that most enemies cannot detect it.

Global Hawk can taxi to the runway, take off, fly to its destination, and come home again without direct human control. It can even land itself. If necessary, the drone can be retasked by its controllers and sent to another area or be told to carry out a new mission.

Although it carries no weapons of its own, the Global Hawk drone helps other forces find their targets and provides detailed information using its cameras, thermal imaging equipment, and radar. Its sophisticated reconnaissance equipment can cover a large area on a single mission, allowing the drone to pass information quickly to forces equipped to act upon it.

The Global Hawk drone is designed to fly to a target area over 930 miles (1,500 km) away, to remain there for a whole day or more, and then return home safely.

Did You Know?

To demonstrate its great range, a Global Hawk was flown nonstop from the United States to Australia, setting several records in the process.

Global Hawk can be used to help intercept vessels carrying drugs, or determine the extent of a disaster like an earthquake or a forest fire.

ZEPHYR

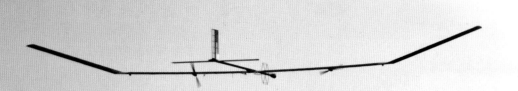

The Zephyr drone looks like a giant model plane, but it is one of the most advanced vehicles ever built. It is solar powered, with batteries that are recharged during the day. Despite its big wingspan, it is very light for its size.

For all its sophistication, the drone is launched by hand and lands on its belly—wheels or other landing gear would be too heavy!

Facts

Zephyr has a very large wingspan, 20 yards (18 m) from wingtip to wingtip. It needs very little power to remain airborne, acting a lot like a glider much of the time.

Zephyr can operate at altitudes of over 13 miles (21 km), above airliner flight paths and even above bad weather. It can stay airborne so long that it can get anywhere it wants to sooner or later, and can stay there for a very long time before returning home.

Zephyr's equipment is carried in a detachable pod. It can carry cameras or thermal imagers for reconnaissance. It can also act as a radio relay station, allowing troops on the ground to use their radios in terrain that might block signals, such as when operating in the mountains.

Zephyr's main job is to monitor a battle area around the clock or to watch for insurgents (rebel fighters) planting bombs. It can help catch drug smugglers or criminals.

HOW BIG IS IT?

Did You Know?

In July 2010 a Zephyr spent two entire weeks in the air without refueling! This is the world record for an unmanned vehicle.

HERON/ HERON TP

The Heron has a main fuselage with a large space available for its equipment package, with twin tail booms. This shape maximizes inside space while keeping the weight down. Heron was designed as a multi-mission platform. This means it can be quickly switched between roles.

Heron has been bought by several nations for military, naval, and policing roles.

Facts

The Heron can fly higher than an airliner. This makes the drone safe to operate even in busy airspace and also reduces the chance that hostiles will detect or attack it.

HOW BIG IS IT?

Did You Know?

Heron's sensors can be manually operated from the ground, or they can be set up to do their job automatically, with a human ready to take over if something important is spotted.

The more advanced Heron TP carries more weight and has more advanced electronics than the basic version.

The original Heron drone can carry up to 550 pounds (250 kg), while the improved TP model hauls 2,200 pounds (1,000 kg). This can include cameras, radar, thermal imagers, and equipment used to intercept signals from enemy radar and radio transmitters. It is also capable of maritime patrol operations, watching an area of sea for hostile vessels or ships that need assistance.

This can be helpful in catching drug smugglers or illegal immigrants.

The Heron drone is designed to be extremely reliable and can operate even in bad weather. It uses automatic systems to take off and land, reducing the chance that an operator will make a mistake and crash the drone at these critical times.

HARFANG

The Harfang drone was developed jointly by France and Israel from the Heron UAV (unmanned aerial vehicle), because France wanted a drone that could be quickly put into service. As a result the Harfang looks a lot like a Heron TP from the outside.

Harfang carries no weapons but has a laser designator, allowing it to pinpoint targets for bombs or missiles fired from other platforms.

HOW BIG IS IT?

A Harfang mission can be 20–24 hours long, during which the drone may be controlled by up to four pilots working in shifts. Normally several other personnel will be directly involved in a mission. These do not fly the drone, but work to quickly make sense of the information it gathers and pass it along to where it can best be used.

Up to 15 technicians are also involved in various aspects of the mission. Some maintain the drone; others make sure the ground control equipment or the sensors aboard the Harfang UAV are working properly.

Did You Know?

The Harfang drone can find its way home if contact with the operators is lost. It will even land itself safely back at base.

The Harfang drone has served in places like Mali and Afghanistan, and was also used in high-profile security operations such as during a visit by the pope.

Facts

Harfang carries cameras, thermal imagers, and radar that allow it to conduct its missions even in bad weather when the ground cannot be seen with ordinary cameras.

PHANTOM EYE

Phantom Eye is designed to operate at high altitude for an extended period of time. It uses advanced hydrogen-powered engines to drive its propellers, giving it a very long range while still allowing it to carry a large payload.

Facts

Phantom Eye can fly at altitudes of almost 21,800 yards (20,000 m), where it is very unlikely to be detected or attacked.

Phantom Eye gets up to flying speed using a cart, so it does not need to carry heavy wheels with it in flight.

Did You Know?

Phantom Eye's engines do not produce any pollution. Their only waste product is water, minimizing the drone's effect on the environment.

HOW BIG IS IT?

Phantom Eye can carry more fuel if it needs to go on a longer mission. In order to hold the extra fuel it is fitted with a bigger fuselage.

Phantom Eye is designed to stay over a target area for days on end at very high altitudes, sending reconnaissance information back to the controllers from its sensor package. It can take video and still images using normal light or infrared, and transmits them home via satellite link.

Phantom Eye was developed from the Condor drone, which set height and endurance records during the 1980s. The Phantom Eye drone has set a record of its own—it is the first fixed-wing drone to use hydrogen fuel cells for power.

APID-55/60

APID-55 is a miniature helicopter that requires very little space to take off and land. It can operate from almost any area of flat ground, so long as there is room for its rotors. An improved version, called APID-60, has also been developed.

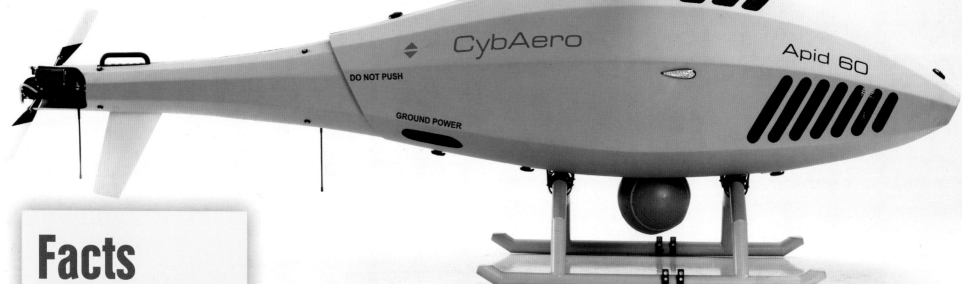

Facts

APID-60 has an endurance of 3—6 hours and a top speed of about 56 miles per hour (90 km/h). It can fly at heights of up to 3,280 yards (3,000 m).

HOW BIG IS IT?

The standard APID-55 uses wheeled landing gear, but an updated version, named APID-60, has been developed with skids instead, like many full-sized helicopters.

The APID-55 was developed by a Swedish company to meet the needs of the United Arab Emirates. Each unit is supplied as three parts: a ground control station, a payload control station that operates the cameras and other equipment aboard the drone, and the drone itself. Contact between the control stations and the drone is by satellite link.

In addition to its use as a military sensor platform, APID-55 can perform a range of civilian missions. These include commercial applications such as monitoring of pipelines in remote areas or surveying large expanses of ground. It can conduct aerial photography, which can be used to make maps or plan construction projects.

Did You Know?

The APID-55 drone can also be used to monitor anything from traffic patterns to forest fires, providing information to planners and responders on the ground.

The APID-60 can be given commands via laptop and will more or less fly itself. The operator can take manual control using a joystick if necessary.

CAMCOPTER S-100

Camcopter S-100 was designed to operate on land or at sea. It had to be able to land on a ship, where there is not much room for mistakes, and to navigate in areas where there are few landmarks.

Camcopter is designed to fly from small warships such as corvettes, which are often too small to operate conventional helicopters.

Camcopter can be used for search-and-rescue operations on land and at sea.

HOW BIG IS IT?

Facts

As well as its cameras, Camcopter S-100 has hardpoints on its sides and two payload bays plus a small electronics bay for any extra equipment it might need.

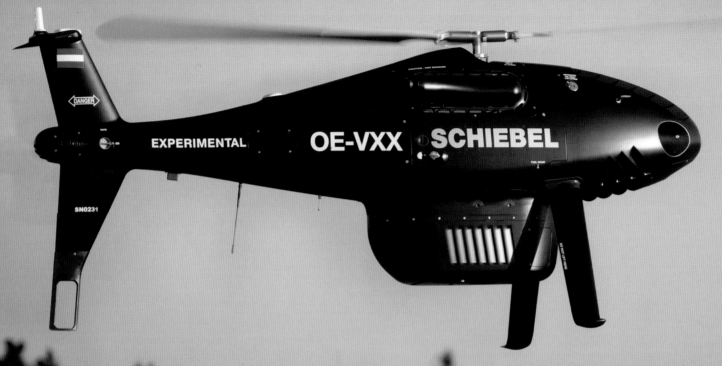

EXPERIMENTAL OE-VXX SCHIEBEL

DANGER

SN0231

Other applications of this small drone range from searching for IEDs (improvised explosive devices) planted by insurgents to patrolling a border to see who is trying to cross.

Did You Know?

Camcopter S-100 has ground-penetrating radar, which can be used to locate mines, as well as other radar systems for use on targets above the surface.

Camcopter S-100 has a navigation computer that uses inertial navigation to find its way around. Inertial navigation means that the drone remembers how it has moved since it took off, and can calculate where it is now relative to its starting point or some other destination.

This is backed up by the GPS system, which tells the drone where it is at any given moment. Even if contact is lost with the GPS system, the drone's computer should be able to figure out where it is and find its way home. Camcopter S-100 can also be operated manually.

MQ-8B FIRE SCOUT

The Fire Scout drone is used by the United States Navy. Being able to take off and land vertically makes it suitable for use aboard small ships.

N398NC
NORTHROP GRUMMAN

Facts

Fire Scout can fly at over 124 miles per hour (200 km/h) and can stay in the air for over 5 hours with a full load. With a lighter load it can fly for up to 8 hours.

HOW BIG IS IT?

Fire Scout's stub wings can be used to carry rockets, missiles, or bombs.

The original design had a three-bladed propeller, but the MQ-8B has a four-bladed design.

Did You Know?

Fire Scout was the first unmanned helicopter to automatically land itself on a moving warship without any human control.

The Fire Scout drone's radar can track multiple contacts at once and can "see" even small boats several miles away.

Fire Scout was developed for the US Navy. When the navy decided it wanted a different drone, the army became interested and a new version was created. This variant met the navy's needs, and the Fire Scout ended up becoming a naval drone after all.

The Fire Scout drone can be armed with Hellfire missiles, Viper Strike laser-guided bombs, or a laser-guided rocket system, but it is mainly intended for reconnaissance and surveillance. It has already been used to help catch fast boats smuggling drugs into the United States.

Falco has a tricycle (three-wheel) undercarriage and needs a runway, though it can be short and does not have to be a very good surface.

FALCO

Falco is a surveillance drone, with cameras but no weaponry. It carries cameras and other sensors that can include thermal imagers, radar equipment, night-vision cameras, and instruments that can detect any use of weapons of mass destruction such as chemical or nuclear weapons.

Facts

Falco can navigate automatically to the target area and back again. It is also capable of automatically watching an area without constant human remote control.

The Falco drone was designed for the government of Pakistan, which needed a reconnaissance and surveillance UAV for military and security purposes. Pakistan is a huge country (it is almost twice the size of California), with many very remote areas, and is sometimes used as a hiding place by insurgents from Afghanistan and elsewhere. A drone fleet allows the government of Pakistan to more effectively watch its borders to see if anyone is sneaking across.

Although designed with operations over Pakistan in mind, the Falco drone was intended to function anywhere and was tested in extremely cold areas with frequent bad weather as well as harsh desert conditions.

The underbelly turret on a Falco drone carries an electro-optical camera and a thermal imager, helping pick out targets in poor light or at night.

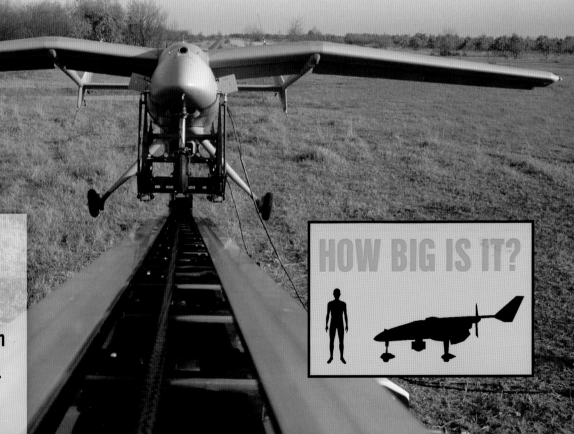

Did You Know?

Basic Falco drones are capable of flying at heights of 5,470 yards (5,000 m) for over 14 hours. A bigger version called Falco EVO can stay airborne for 18 hours or more.

HOW BIG IS IT?

PHOENIX

The Phoenix drone was developed in the early 1980s for the British Army. It was used for years, then retired in 2006. Although official government statements say that Phoenix was effective and popular, those who had to operate the drone report that it had many problems.

Facts

Phoenix was driven by a propeller at the front. This meant that its cameras and other equipment had to be mounted in a pod slung under the drone's belly.

The underslung camera pod gave Phoenix good all-around vision, but meant that the drone could not land on its belly without damaging it.

Many Phoenix drones were lost, either by being damaged on landing or by failing to return from their missions. If you lose control of a drone over enemy territory, you're probably not going to get it back! This is what happened to a lot of Phoenix drones over the Balkans and Iraq in the 1990s.

Some Phoenix drones were intentionally sacrificed when their operators deliberately kept them over enemy territory until they no longer had enough fuel to get home. This kind of sacrifice is expensive, but drones can be replaced and sometimes losing one was necessary to get the job done.

HOW BIG IS IT?

Did You Know

To protect its camera pod, Phoenix landed upside down! It was fitted with an airbag to prevent damage to the drone and its equipment.

Phoenix could land almost anywhere. It could also take off in a very short space, as it was launched from a rail mounted on a truck.

RANGER

Ranger is a twin-boom tail UAV launched from a hydraulic catapult. It is used by Finland and Switzerland. Swiss Ranger drones belong to the air force, but they are sometimes used to help out the police.

Ranger uses a modular payload system, allowing its equipment to be quickly swapped.

The twin-boom tail is a common feature of UAVs. It provides good stability without adding much weight.

Facts

Ranger can fly at heights of over 5,468 yards (5,000 m) for up to 9 hours. It carries a forward-looking infrared (FLIR) camera system in a turret under the fuselage.

Ranger's design features long straight wings, central fuselage, and twin-boom tail. This allows the drone to be pushed by a propeller mounted on the back of the fuselage, which in turn means that cameras and other equipment can be mounted at the front where they can look forward as well as sideways.

Ranger is launched from a hydraulic catapult, which means it can take off from almost anywhere with no need for a runway. It does need level ground to land on, but any strip of grass or concrete will do. The drone can also be put down in snow or on firm ice if necessary.

In an emergency it is possible to launch a drone even though there is nowhere for it to land. Nobody would do that with a manned aircraft, but drones are expendable if necessary.

Did You Know?

The Ranger drone normally lands on the ground like a plane but if necessary it can use a parachute to bring itself down safely.

HOW BIG IS IT?

RQ-7 SHADOW

The RQ-7 Shadow drone is in service with the US Marine Corps and US Army. It is used for reconnaissance, to find targets, and to assess the amount of damage done to the enemy by an attack.

RQ-7 Shadow is launched from a rail mounted on a trailer towed by a light vehicle such as a HMMMV (Humvee).

Facts

Early Shadow drones were designated RQ-7A, but these have been replaced with more advanced RQ-7B models that carry improved sensors and electronics.

HOW BIG IS IT?

Shadow drones can be launched from almost anywhere their trailer-mounted launcher can park, and can land on any flat surface. The original RQ-7A could stay in the air for about 5.5 hours, but the bigger, improved RQ-7B version can fly for 6 or 7 hours. A new wing design increases this to up to 9 hours.

The Shadow drone carries infrared and television cameras in a ball-shaped turret under the main fuselage. It can also carry radar or communications packages or other equipment including a laser rangefinder and designator, instruments that are used to guide bombs and missiles to their targets.

The RQ-7 Shadow drone uses a twin-boom tail section with an angled tailplane to keep it clear of the "pusher" propeller.

Did You Know?

Shadow drones have clocked up hundreds of thousands of flight-hours in service. This is a measure of how long the drones have spent in the air since they began operations.

PUMA

Puma looks just like a toy plane, with a twin-bladed propeller at the front. It has a maximum range of 9.3 miles (15 km) and can stay aloft for 2 hours, using power supplied by a rechargeable fuel cell.

HOW BIG IS IT?

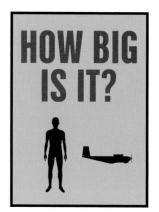

Puma's sensors can swivel to point in any direction, keeping the target under surveillance no matter which way the drone is facing.

Facts

Puma needs no equipment to launch or to be recovered. It is thrown into the air, and it can land on water or any flat ground.

With a top speed of 51 miles per hour (83 kmh), the Puma drone is slower than many cars, but it does not have to deal with obstacles on the ground.

Puma is a small drone capable of carrying cameras and thermal imaging equipment to a height of about 164 yards (150 m). It was designed for both civilian and military operations, and can be used at sea. Its sensor package is waterproof and will survive a wet landing.

Puma can be used to "eyeball" suspect vessels at sea or to provide boarding teams with an idea of what to expect aboard a ship as they approach. Its cameras can capture screenshots as well as playing video, making the drone useful for gathering evidence for law-enforcement purposes.

Did You Know?

Puma can be manually controlled or can navigate by itself using GPS. It can also land itself when the mission is over.

RQ-14 DRAGON EYE

Dragon Eye is a small UAV driven by two propellers. Its motors are electric, which makes it much quieter than larger drones that rely on combustion engines, and its small size makes it unlikely to be spotted.

Dragon Eye is made from lightweight materials, much like Styrofoam.

Dragon Eye's two propellers are driven by electric motors.

HOW BIG IS IT?

Dragon Eye is a small drone with a short range. It can be launched by hand or catapulted into the air with a bungee cord. Once airborne, the drone can be manually controlled or it can fly through a series of preprogrammed waypoints (locations along a flight path). Its batteries last for about an hour of flight.

Dragon Eye weighs just 5.5 pounds (2.5 kg), plus another 1.1 pounds (0.5 kg) for its camera. The drone is made up of five main parts, which are designed to fit into a backpack for easy carrying. It takes about 10 minutes to put it together before a mission.

There are plans to upgrade Dragon Eye, giving it better sensors and a longer-lasting battery that will increase its range and the time it can spend out on a mission.

Facts

Dragon Eye carries a sideways-looking camera that can produce a good picture even in very poor light conditions. There are plans to fit it with alternative sensors.

Did You Know?

Dragon Eye is very simple to operate, so it takes just a week to train the operator.

RQ-11 RAVEN

The Raven drone is a short-range UAV used by the US Army for operations including convoy security (helping protect vehicles on the move by watching for enemies in the area), reconnaissance during urban operations, and to help protect forces in the field by providing them with an all-around view of the tactical situation.

HOW BIG IS IT?

Raven is driven by a pusher propeller that is mounted high on the rear of the main fuselage.

Raven has no landing gear, but it is so light that it does not need any. It just lands on its belly.

Facts

Raven is the most common small drone used by US forces. It is hand-launched and can stay in the air for 60–90 minutes.

Raven mounts a video camera in the nose, along with an infrared camera, and a second infrared camera facing sideways. One of the variants available has an alternative nose with a special camera capable of looking in any direction.

Raven can stay airborne for up to 90 minutes and has a range of 7.5 miles (12 km). It can reach altitudes of up to 4,920 yards (4,500 m) during a mission, or can stay low if necessary. It cannot fly very fast, but it does not need to cover large distances so this does not matter very much.

The Raven drone sends pictures back to the operator in real time. This means he or she can see what's going on as it happens without delay.

Did You Know?

Raven has been successfully used by the US Army during urban combat operations, spotting hostiles that might have been impossible to see from ground level.

SCANEAGLE

ScanEagle is a small reconnaissance drone in service with the US Armed Forces and the Australian Army. It is designed to help protect vessels at sea and important installations on land by monitoring the area around them for threats.

Facts

ScanEagle is built in five sections: the nose, the fuselage, the wings, the propulsion system, and the electronics segment. A damaged section can be changed quickly.

ScanEagle is normally launched from a catapult system, though it can also be dropped by an aircraft such as a C-130 Hercules.

A ScanEagle can be recovered by flying it into a suspended "snagging line" that catches on hooks at the drone's wingtips.

The drone can also land on an area of flat ground, though it has no wheels or other landing gear.

Did You Know?

ScanEagle can be modified for operations in cold weather, with coverings that prevent ice from forming on the wings. If too much ice builds up, the drone would become heavy and could be forced down.

ScanEagle's long wings and small fuselage give it a lot of lift, letting the drone fly for an extended period without using much power. It has a stabilized turret in its nose to carry sensors including cameras and infrared systems that can stay locked onto a target no matter what the drone is doing.

The drone can carry specialist sensors to detect chemical weapons or other harmful chemicals, as well as a magnetic detector that can be used to locate metal objects underwater or hidden on land. It can also carry a device that helps locate enemy snipers.

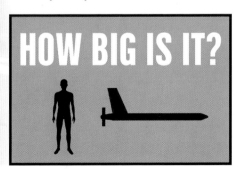

HOW BIG IS IT?

MAVERIC

Maveric is a small modular UAV capable of day or night operations. Its small size and unusual design make it unlikely to be spotted or recognized as a drone; Maveric can easily be mistaken for a bird.

Maveric's wings resemble those of a bird. They are light and flexible, making them hard to damage.

The wings have a carbon-fiber frame covered in tough fabric.

Facts

Maveric is put together as several carbon-fiber modules. The wings can be bent, allowing the drone to be carried in a tube-shaped pouch.

HOW BIG IS IT?

Maveric has a sensor position in its nose that normally mounts a camera, and a belly-mounted pod that can carry a range of payloads. The payload is often a second camera or thermal imager. The pod-mounted camera can swivel to give full 360-degree coverage.

The drone's software makes images from its cameras less shaky before they are transmitted, and if the drone is out of communications range with its operators, it can store images until it is back in contact. While it is out of contact, Maveric is designed to fly on its own, without remote control. This drone needs very little human input during its mission.

Did You Know?
This drone can take care of itself. Maveric's onboard electronics are programmed to avoid collisions with objects on its flight path.

Maveric's wing design helps it cope with gusty winds. It can be launched in gusts of up to 35 knots (40 miles per hour; 65 kmh) without crashing.

DESERT HAWK

Desert Hawk is a small UAV in use with the US Air Force and the British Army. It is small enough to be carried dismantled in a backpack and weighs less than 6.6 pounds (3 kg) empty.

Desert Hawk is mostly made of plastic foam, which makes it look like a toy but is very light and tough.

Facts

Desert Hawk was developed to meet an urgent need for a drone that could help keep US Air Force bases secure. Its primary role was to watch the area around the base for intruders and other possible threats.

Desert Hawk is powered by a pusher propeller driven by an electric motor. Its batteries are good for about 60 minutes of flight, after which they have to be recharged. It is extremely quiet and might not be noticed by hostiles in the area. It has three cameras and mostly flies itself, though an operator can retask the drone whenever necessary.

Desert Hawk has also seen service with the US Army, where it was used for airborne surveillance to help protect both bases and convoys moving through potentially hostile territory in Iraq and Afghanistan.

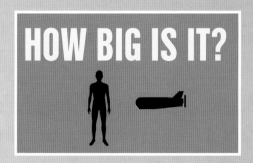

HOW BIG IS IT?

Did You Know?

Desert Hawk was eventually replaced by the more advanced Desert Hawk III, which saw active service in Afghanistan with the British Army.

Desert Hawk is launched using a bungee cord, which can be secured to any suitable fixed object. It lands on its belly and skids to a stop.

Dragonfly is designed to be simple to fly and does not need much room to operate, enabling the user to stay concealed from the enemy.

HOW BIG IS IT?

DRAGONFLY

Dragonfly is a quadrotor military drone used for surveillance and reconnaissance work. It is designed to work with other drones as part of an advanced battle-management system that helps friendly units know where their allies are and thus avoid incidents where troops accidentally shoot at their own side.

Facts

Dragonfly uses four rotors for stability. It is designed to be as "soldier proof" (meaning hard to break) as possible so it can survive on the battlefield.

Did You Know?

Dragonfly can be controlled using a vest with electronic systems built in that can be operated by the soldier wearing it.

Dragonfly was designed to be just one part of an integrated electronic system called FELIN, which provides support to troops on the battlefield. Drones like Dragonfly are used to watch the combat area and to keep track of friendly units ("blue forces") and hostile troops ("red forces").

This knowledge of the battlefield allows commanders to plan the movement of their forces very precisely, avoiding contact with the enemy when necessary and fighting only when they have an advantage. Support weapons such as artillery, missiles, and mortars can be aimed to come down exactly where they are most needed, even very close to friendly troops, without risking the possibility of hitting the wrong targets.

Dragonfly is just one of several drone systems that can be controlled by the FELIN Tactical Tablet.

ALADIN

The Aladin drone looks like a high-tech version of a classic model aircraft. It can be carried easily by a soldier on foot, and is in service with German and Dutch forces for short-range reconnaissance.

Aladin can be quickly assembled and is launched either using a bungee cord or simply by throwing it.

HOW BIG IS IT?

Facts

Aladin typically flies 32–328 yards (30–300 m) above the ground, but can go as high as 4,920 yards (4,500 m). It cruises at 25–43 miles per hour (40–70 km/h) and carries four cameras for reconnaissance work.

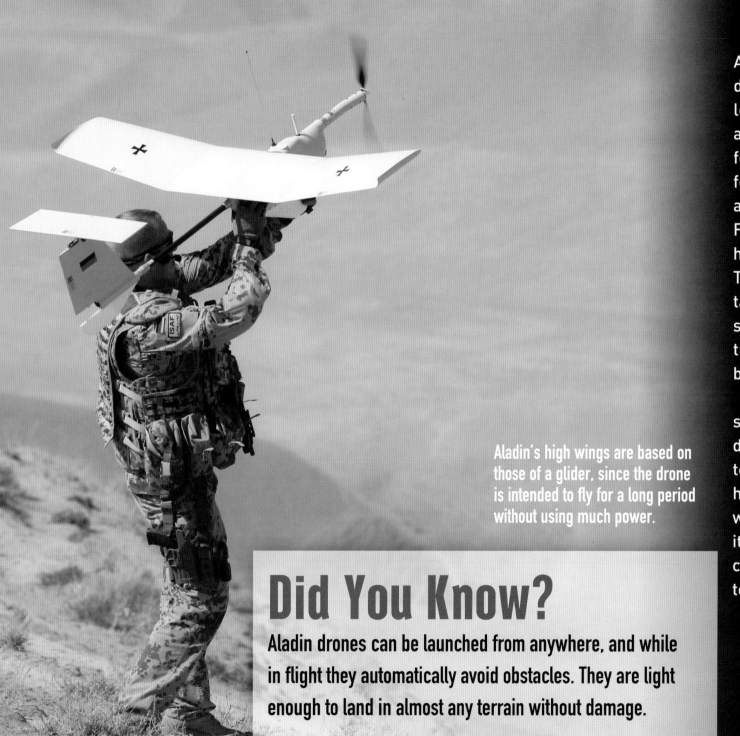

Aladin is a small, lightweight drone designed to provide local-area reconnaissance at short notice. It carries four cameras: one pointing forward, two downward, and one pointed sideways. For nighttime work it also has a thermal imager. These cameras are used to take different views of the surrounding area and can transmit still or video images back to base.

Aladin is piloted by setting up a series of three-dimensional waypoints that tell the drone where and how high to go next. Between waypoints the drone pilots itself, but the operator can cancel some and add others to change the mission.

Aladin's high wings are based on those of a glider, since the drone is intended to fly for a long period without using much power.

Did You Know?

Aladin drones can be launched from anywhere, and while in flight they automatically avoid obstacles. They are light enough to land in almost any terrain without damage.

X-51 WAVERIDER

WaveRider is an experimental hypersonic aircraft. It can fly at incredibly high speeds, over five times the speed of sound. WaveRider holds the record for the longest hypersonic flight ever made, and is being used to develop a new generation of extremely fast missiles.

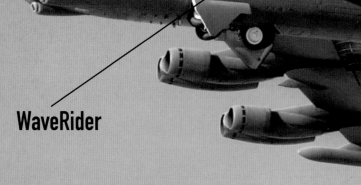

WaveRider

WaveRider uses a rocket booster to reach Mach 4.5 (the ratio of speed of the aircraft to the speed of air that its moving in) and then switches to it's own engine.

The drone needs only tiny wings because of its high speed.

Facts

WaveRider can fly at altitudes of over 23,000 yards (21,000 m) and has a range of 466 miles (750 km). Its purpose is to let scientists learn about extremely high-speed flight.

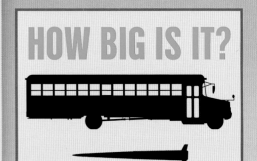

HOW BIG IS IT?

WaveRider is launched from a bomber at high altitude and accelerates using a rocket booster. When it is going fast enough, its own "scramjet" (supersonic ramjet) engine takes over. This kind of engine requires high speeds to operate.

A missile called High Speed Strike Weapon (HSSW) is planned, and it will be based on WaveRider. The idea behind the development of the HSSW is that a missile that goes fast enough cannot be shot down. Enemy targets might not even see it coming.

WaveRider can get to its target much quicker than a normal missile, making a hit far more likely.

The JP-7 fuel used by WaveRider was developed for the Mach 3 capable SR-71 Blackbird aircraft.

Did You Know?

WaveRider got its name because it creates shock waves as it travels through the air, and uses them to provide lift instead of conventional wings.

BQM-74 CHUKAR

BQM-74 Chukar is basically a missile with no warhead (the part of the missile that explodes and damages the target) that provides a realistic target for guns and missiles. It is designed to be recovered and used again after an exercise, making military exercises more cost-effective.

Facts

The Chukar drone can be programmed to fly at up to 13,120 yards (12,000 m) or close to the sea, and can reach speeds of around 590 miles per hour (950 km/h).

HOW BIG IS IT?

The BQM-74 Chukar can be used as a target for "live" defensive weapons, but this will destroy the drone. More commonly defensive missiles are fitted with a transmitter that shows how close they got to the target drone, and gunfire uses inert projectiles that are tracked by radar. So long as the defensive fire was in the right place at the right time, "live" weapons would stop a missile.

Some drones were converted for use as decoys during the 1991 Gulf War. Launched at Iraqi targets, they drew a response that showed Coalition planners where the enemy air defenses were strongest.

BQM-74 Chukar is powered by a turbojet engine that can keep it in the air for over an hour.

Chukar is normally launched from a rail aboard a ship, using two boosters strapped under the wings.

An adapter kit allows the drone to be launched from an aircraft instead.

Did You Know?

The Chukar drone has flotation tanks to keep it afloat if it crashes in the sea. It can then easily be recovered and reused.

HOW BIG IS IT?

FIREBEE

The first Firebee target drone flew in 1951. Since then, several versions of the drone have been used for training and as targets for weapon systems such as the Stinger ground-to-air missile.

Facts

From 1970 to 1973, modified Firebee drones flew over 250 reconnaissance missions, intercepting radio signals.

Firebee drones can be launched from a DC-130 Hercules, which can carry two drones under each wing.

When a Firebee has completed its mission it descends on a parachute and is caught by a helicopter that snags the chute.

The Firebee drone has had a long service history and has been adapted several times. It was modified to enable it to mimic a larger aircraft, and it was given advanced electronic systems so that it could dodge like a manned fighter when under fire. Firebee drones carry flares on the wingtips that cause missiles to destroy the easily replaced wings instead of the expensive engine.

Some Firebees were converted to surveillance drones, monitoring North Korean radio transmissions in 1970–73. These drones were given modifications designed to make them hard to detect on radar, making them some of the first stealth aircraft ever flown.

Firebee drones can also be launched from a ground station with the assistance of a rocket booster mounted under the tail section.

Did You Know?

Firebees can be reused many times. This means that the same drone might get shot down over and over again for years on end, but as long as it isn't shot down over enemy territory, it can be used again.

PATHFINDER

Pathfinder is a solar-powered drone aircraft capable of staying airborne for a very long time. It started out as a technology demonstrator but was later converted for high-altitude scientific missions that could reach as high as 78,740 feet (24,000 m), the length of about 220 football fields.

Facts

Pathfinder is powered by solar cells located on the top of its wing. It has batteries for times when there is no sunlight to power its motors.

Pathfinder started out with eight motors.
Two were removed, leaving six.

Pathfinder's wing is so delicate that it bends under the drone's very light weight.

HOW BIG IS IT?

Pathfinder started out as an experimental aircraft, to see what could be done with solar-powered planes. It was then developed into a scientific research craft that could stay up in the highest part of the atmosphere for days on end. It was further modified to create Pathfinder Plus, which had a longer wing and held more solar panels.

Pathfinder has been used to monitor forests and coastal regions, collecting data on how well the area was recovering from a hurricane or how the climate varied over time. It has also been used in experiments testing whether high-altitude drones can be used instead of communications satellites.

Did You Know?

Pathfinder steers by controlling the speed of the motors on one side, pulling the drone around rather than guiding it with a rudder.

The original Pathfinder design had only part of the upper wing surface covered in solar panels, but now the whole surface is used.

CENTURION

Centurion was developed from the smaller Pathfinder drone. It is larger, with a longer wing that can carry more solar cells to gather energy for its instruments and its 14 electric motors. Its electronic systems are carried in pods under the wing.

Centurion is a larger, more advanced version of the Pathfinder drone.

A larger wing means more room for solar panels, and thus more power.

Facts

Centurion can reach heights of up to 19 miles (30 km) above the earth's surface while carrying almost 660 pounds (300 kg) of scientific instruments, and can stay there for days or even weeks.

The Centurion drone was developed as part of NASA's ERAST (Environmental Research Aircraft and Sensor Technology) program. One of the project goals was to create an aircraft that could fly high enough to study the ozone layer, and to stay airborne long enough to track changes over a long period.

A smaller version of Centurion was built to test the design before the full-size drone was launched. Even then, at first it flew on battery power so that the expensive solar panels would not be damaged if Centurion crashed. The panels were only fitted once the design was shown to work.

It is hoped that eventually solar-powered aircraft will be able to stay in the air for months at a time. Centurion is a step in this direction.

Did You Know?
Centurion was tested with an anvil as cargo instead of expensive scientific instruments.

HOW BIG IS IT?

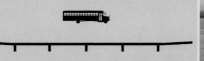

CROPCAM

CropCam is a radio-controlled aircraft fitted with a camera and a GPS receiver. It is designed to help farmers monitor their land, showing dry areas or vegetation patterns that might not be obvious from the ground.

CropCam uses a battery-powered electric motor. It can remain airborne for nearly an hour.

HOW BIG IS IT?

Facts

CropCam uses GPS to automatically take a series of photos as it flies over a field. These individual photos can be combined to make a larger image.

CropCam can fly in winds of up to 19 miles per hour (30 kmh), but high winds may affect the quality of picture it takes.

CropCam uses standard remote-control plane components that are easily available and help keep the costs down.

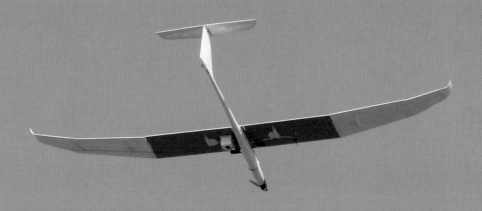

Did You Know?

CropCam is tough, but if it gets damaged it can be fixed by swapping out parts from a remote-control plane.

Aerial photographs are extremely useful to farmers, but they are expensive to obtain. Few farmers could afford to take a set of photos every week. CropCam allows the user to do just that. It is launched by simply throwing it into the air, and costs virtually nothing to operate.

CropCam's photos help a farmer to spot damage from pests, disease, or other troubles, early. The user can make an assessment of the size of the problem area, and then decide what to do about it. Forestry companies can also use CropCam to monitor acres of forest land.

MAJA

MAJA looks a lot like a model plane, with a pusher propeller at the rear. Its main fuselage is designed to carry as much as possible. A large hatch running along most of its length gives access to the interior.

MAJA's fuselage is designed to hold as much as possible.

The top-mounted hatch gives easy access to the cargo area.

Facts

MAJA can carry up to 3.3 pounds (1.5 kg) of cameras and other equipment, and can be fitted with different-sized wings depending on its mission and payload.

The MAJA drone was designed for aerial photography and surveying, particularly in the field of environmental protection. It was designed for ruggedness, as it would have to operate in some very remote areas with little chance of repair if it became damaged.

MAJA drones are used in various conservation projects worldwide. Their cameras and other sensors can collect information on animals living in wild and remote areas that are not accessible to people on foot. Also, the drone is less likely to scare off the animals it is trying to observe.

Did You Know?

The MAJA drone has been used to film orangutans in the forests of Sumatra.

HOW BIG IS IT?

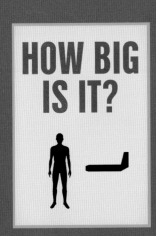

The MAJA drone can stay airborne for about an hour with a load of about 3.3 pounds (1.5 kg).

SCOUT

Scout is a quadcopter drone designed to help farmers and other agricultural producers monitor fields and crops. It is built from carbon fiber, which is both light and strong. It has a range of about 0.93 miles (1.5 km).

Facts

Scout is designed to take both video and still images using a stabilized camera that remains steady on target even when the drone is moving fast.

Scout's long rotor booms are designed to keep its rotors out of sight of the camera so that they do not interfere with pictures.

Scout can fly for up to 20 minutes, taking images of a much greater area than the user could observe in the same time.

Scout is a low-cost drone designed to be easily operated and quickly made ready for flight. It is stabilized to stay level in flight, and it can be commanded to automatically hover in place or to follow the user as he or she walks. If the drone runs low on power it automatically returns to base at a preset height. At this height it should avoid most obstacles.

The operator can save a flight plan and reuse it later, allowing a set of images of exactly the same place to be built up over time. This can help show changes before they become too serious.

HOW BIG IS IT?

Did You Know?

Scout's camera can be remotely controlled by the operator, pivoting up to 90 degrees to focus on any area in its field of view.

OCTANE

Octane is a short-range mini-drone designed as a four-rotor quadcopter with a central hub containing electronics, batteries, and flight controls. It can carry out a wide range of missions, from crop monitoring to disaster assessment and aerial photography.

Octane can carry different payloads under its main central section.

How much load is carried affects the drone's range and flying time.

Facts

With a 1.1-pounds (0.5 kg) load, Octane can reach a target 1.2 miles (2 km) away, take photos for a minute or so, and get back to base.

HOW BIG IS IT?

The Octane drone can carry a maximum load of 1.1 pounds (0.5 kg), which limits flying time to about 18 minutes. It can stay airborne longer with a smaller load. The drone has many uses. Farmers might use it to monitor their crops, while geologists and archaeologists can search for interesting sites much more quickly than if they had to walk in search of the sites.

The drone can also be used to monitor sports events and other situations where large crowds gather, and it can be sent into an area threatened by fire or chemical spills to assess the situation without putting people at risk.

Did You Know?

When the Octane drone is operating near obstacles it can be fitted with a guard to prevent the propellers from being damaged if they hit something.

Small UAVs like Octane are almost completely silent and hard to spot, making them unlikely to upset local wildlife if used in the countryside.

Wave Sight is launched from a rail using compressed gas to get it up to flying speed.

WAVE SIGHT

Wave Sight is a small, fixed-wing UAV with a wingspan of 2.5 yards (2.3 m). It is less than 1.6 yards (1.5 m) long from nose to tail but can carry a variety of payloads, up to a maximum of 4.4 pounds (2 kg).

Facts

Wave Sight can be set up in about 15 minutes and can be ready for another mission in just 5 minutes.

Wave Sight's large wings and twin tail fins give it plenty of lift and keep it stable in flight, enabling the drone to carry large payloads for its size. The payload is carried inside the main fuselage and the wings. Maximum flying time is about 30 minutes with a 4.4-pounds (2 kg) load, but with a lighter payload aboard (less than 0.6 pounds, or 0.3 kg) the drone can fly for 2 hours.

Payload can be quickly swapped for a different load, and the drone is designed to be quickly relaunched for another mission once it is recovered. It can also be retasked while in the air.

HOW BIG IS IT?

Wave Sight is powered by an electric motor driving a front-mounted propeller.

Did You Know?

Wave Sight can land almost anywhere because it is very light, but if necessary it can also bring itself down with a parachute.

EBEE

The eBee drone is a small, lightweight, and easily portable mini-UAV capable of creating extremely detailed maps of the ground or photomosaics built out of thousands of images taken through its camera.

eBee can be used to create extremely accurate maps of the area below using its onboard camera.

HOW BIG IS IT?

Facts

eBee has a wingspan of just under 1 yard (1 m), but once the detachable wings are taken off, the whole drone fits in a small case.

The eBee drone carries an extremely powerful camera, which is used not just to map the ground but also to tell the drone when it is getting too low. The drone will automatically climb when it gets too close to the ground, and in other dangerous situations it is programmed to return to base. The eBee needs just 5.5 yards (5 m) of landing area.

eBees download their data into a computer package that builds a detailed map out of the images. These maps are highly useful to scientists, geologists, mining engineers, mountaineers, and anyone else who needs to know how the land lies.

Did You Know?

The eBee's engine is started by shaking it three times. After that it is launched by simply throwing it by hand.

eBee drones have been used to build an extremely accurate map of the Matterhorn, a mountain between Switzerland and Italy.

Precision Hawk is used by farmers to monitor how well their crops are doing and to identify problem areas in time to do something about them.

PRECISION HAWK

Precision Hawk is a small fixed-wing UAV that can carry a range of advanced sensors. It can take off from and land on water using a set of small floats as landing gear, and it can operate automatically with no need for human input.

Facts

Precision Hawk is less than 1 yard (1 m) long from nose to tail. It weighs about 3.3 pounds (1.5 kg), but can carry a wide range of sensors.

The Precision Hawk drone can carry a range of sensor equipment for many different missions. It monitors the quality of the images it takes while in flight, and it can retake an image that has not come out well. The drone's software uploads its sensor data to a cloud for immediate processing, and the user can look at what the drone is monitoring in real-time.

Precision Hawk drones can be used to monitor fairly long-term situations like water quality, mining, and agriculture, and they can also provide data quickly in an emergency such as a search-and-rescue operation by sending it straight to the user's tablet or laptop.

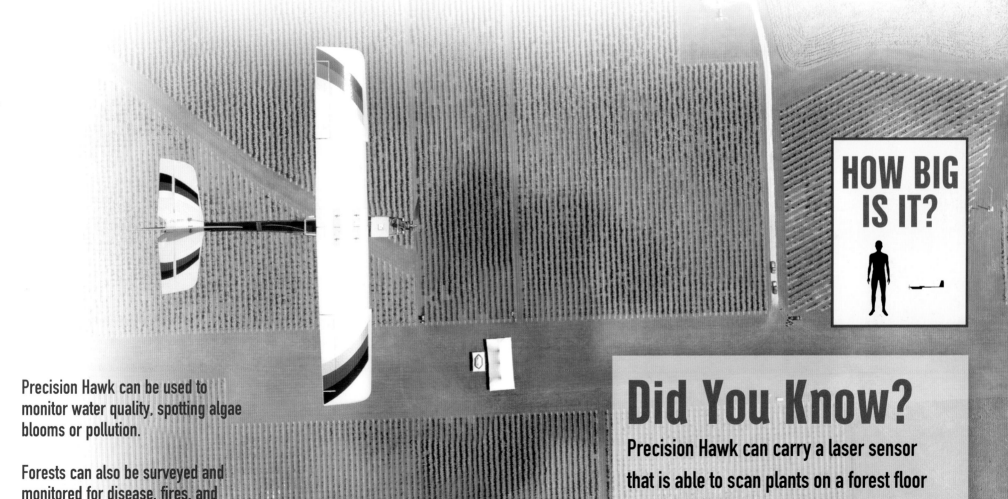

HOW BIG IS IT?

Precision Hawk can be used to monitor water quality, spotting algae blooms or pollution.

Forests can also be surveyed and monitored for disease, fires, and general health.

Did You Know?

Precision Hawk can carry a laser sensor that is able to scan plants on a forest floor through the leaves of the trees above.

PRIME AIR

Prime Air is an eight-rotor drone designed to deliver small packages of up to 5.5 pounds (2.5 kg) weight over distances of about 9.3 miles (15 km). It could enter service as soon as 2015.

Prime Air consists of a lifting section and a package carried underneath.

Facts

The main obstacle to getting Prime Air into service is not making the drone work—it already does. The problem is that new laws are needed to govern the use of delivery drones, and these must be in place before the system can be launched.

HOW BIG IS IT?

The drone has eight sets of rotors; two sets along each of its sides. All the rotor sets are powered from the central section.

Prime Air's operators say that their drone delivery system is ready to go as soon as the law gives permission to start operations.

Air traffic of all kinds is strictly regulated by laws that prevent pilots flying about as they please, and these laws do not allow unmanned aircraft to operate in built-up areas. In order for delivery drones to be used, new laws have to be put in place that spell out how the drones are to operate and how they are to be made safe.

A main requirement is redundancy—that is, if a component of a drone fails it will not simply fall out of the sky and hit someone. Reliability is also important—the package has to get to the right place!

Did You Know?

Prime Air is designed to pick up packages from a conveyor belt and deliver them directly to the consumer. The whole process is automated as part of the ordering system.

Facts

Remus can operate at depths of up to 109 yards (100 m), and for up to 10 hours depending on what equipment is being carried.

The torpedo-like shape glides easily through water and has plenty of space inside for equipment.

REMUS

The Remus AUV (autonomous underwater vehicle) looks a lot like a torpedo, but instead of explosives it can carry a range of instruments and equipment for underwater work. It is part of a "family" of underwater drones that can all be customized for various missions.

Remus can carry a range of sensors, depending on what mission is being undertaken.

HOW BIG IS IT?

Remus is a coastal AUV used by the military as well as oil companies, shipbuilders, harbor operators, and police. It mounts cameras and lights on a turret that can swivel to look in any direction, finding debris that might endanger a ship or cracks in an underwater pipeline.

Remus can also carry sonar systems for use in locating wrecks, mapping the seabed, finding mines, or studying fish. It is small and light enough for two people to be able to carry it when out of the water, and it is so simple to operate that an operator can be trained in just a few days.

The Remus AUV is designed so that equipment can be swapped out between missions or when a better sensor becomes available.

Did You Know?

The US Navy uses Remus drones to find mines and to map shallow waters where a large vessel might run into trouble.

DEEP TREKKER

Deep Trekker is a family of mini-ROVs (remotely operated vehicle), or very small vehicles intended to carry cameras and other equipment. These ROVs are inexpensive, and they are aimed at a very wide range of users including people who want to explore underwater, just for fun.

Facts

Deep Trekker is powered by internal batteries and can operate for about 6—8 hours between recharges. It can operate in depths of up to 82 yards (75 m).

Deep Trekker's camera can move inside the body or can be locked in place so that it can be aimed by pivoting the drone.

Deep Trekker uses a pair of thrusters to move underwater. Their direction is controlled by turning the whole drone.

HOW BIG IS IT?

Deep Trekker is operated by a console-like controller, with a display screen to see what the camera is looking at. The controller is small enough that the user can move around or even pass it to other people. The drone is connected to the user by a tether, so if it becomes stuck or the battery runs out it can be dragged out of the water by hand.

The basic Deep Trekker carries a camera, but accessories are available including a grabber that can be used to pick up objects underwater, a compact sonar package, and a device for taking samples of underwater sediment.

Deep Trekker can be used for underwater inspections and work, or even for underwater filming.

Did You Know?

Deep Trekker can carry a fishing line and take it to where the fish are. When one takes the bait, the line detaches from the ROV and is reeled in as usual.

HYDROVIEW

HydroView is a small ROV consisting of a central camera pod and two side-mounted thrusters. It is capable of a speed of 5 knots (5.8 miles per hour; 9.3 kmh) underwater and can reach a depth of about 50 yards (45 m).

Facts

HydroView is designed to be extremely simple to operate. It can be controlled using a laptop or the motion control capability of an iPad.

HOW BIG IS IT?

HydroView's camera can take HD video and feed it straight to the operator, or take still pictures.

The small ROV can be easily stored aboard a boat until it is needed.

HydroView is a small, inexpensive ROV designed to meet a range of needs. It can be used to inspect boats for damage without needing to get in the water, or to look for a dive site such as a wreck so that divers can enter the water in the right place.

HydroView can record several minutes of high-quality underwater footage or display it in real-time on a laptop or tablet. Engineers can send a HydroView to check out underwater systems, then look over the video to see what needs to be done; all of this can be done without anyone having to go in the water.

Did You Know?
The "topside box" that controls the HydroView supplies Wi-Fi for use with a tablet or laptop.

HydroView is small enough to get into confined spaces that a diver might not be able to enter safely.

VIDEORAY PRO 4

VideoRay is a small, computer-controlled ROV capable of operating at depths of up to 328 yards (300 m). It carries a camera in its main pressure hull and can be fitted with additional equipment including a sonar package.

Facts

VideoRay can be transported and deployed by a single operator. It operates at the end of a tether that also carries control signals.

VideoRay looks like a miniature submarine, with thrusters at the rear.

VideoRay's camera is located in the central pressure hull, where it is protected from damage.

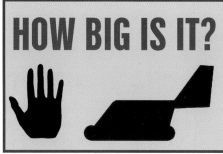

HOW BIG IS IT?

VideoRay can be used to inspect underwater objects such as oil pipelines or the inside of water tanks. It can operate in deep water that would require special equipment for human divers.

Military and law enforcement users can search for mines or for illegal substances being carried outside a ship's hull without sending down divers.

VideoRay's tether is very strong. It is possible to retrieve objects of over 88 pounds (40 kg) by grabbing them with the ROV's manipulator arm and pulling the object and the ROV out of the water with the tether.

VideoRay can carry a range of accessories including a manipulator arm and a device to allow it to crawl along a ship's hull.

Did You Know?

Scuba divers are advised against diving deeper than 32 yards (30 m). VideoRay can go 10 times deeper without coming to harm.

Facts

Bluefin-21 AUV can stay underwater for 25 hours, carrying out a wide range of missions, and can dive to depths of 4,920 yards (4,500 m) or more.

Bluefin can be launched using a crane or hoist from almost any kind of vessel.

Bluefin is built in sections that can be swapped to set up the drone for different missions.

BLUEFIN-21

Bluefin-21 is part of a family of torpedo-shaped AUVs that can carry out a range of missions. It is normally used for civilian applications but can hunt for mines and unexploded bombs if necessary.

The Bluefin drone is built from modules that can be replaced when the drone has a different job to do. The drone has two computers: one to operate the drone itself and another to control the payload. When a different set of sensors or equipment is fitted, it communicates with this computer, which in turn communicates with the main computer.

Bluefin can operate at great depths, making it highly useful in examining underwater pipes or searching for wrecks on the seabed. It can map possible archaeological sites and other areas of interest or carry sensors for environmental research.

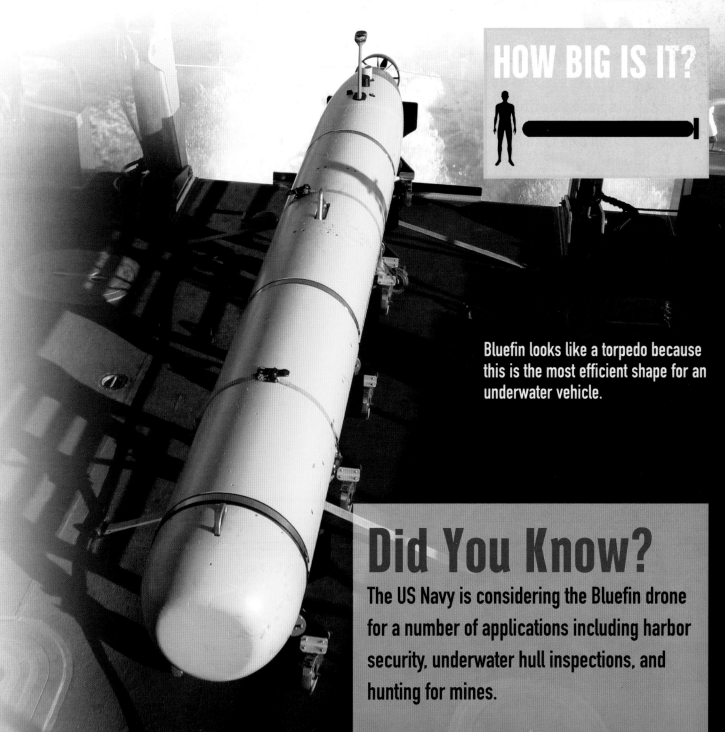

HOW BIG IS IT?

Bluefin looks like a torpedo because this is the most efficient shape for an underwater vehicle.

Did You Know?

The US Navy is considering the Bluefin drone for a number of applications including harbor security, underwater hull inspections, and hunting for mines.

INDEX